Workbook

For

Dr. Gladys McGarey's

The Well-Lived Life

Smart Reads

Note to readers:
This is an unofficial workbook for Dr. Gladys McGarey's "The Well-Lived Life" designed to enrich your reading experience. The original book can be purchased on Amazon.

Download Your Free Gift

As a way to say "Thank You" for being a fan of our series, I've included a free gift for you:

Brain Health: How to Nurture and Nourish Your Brain For Top Performance

Go to www.smart-reads.com to get your FREE book.

The Smart Reads Team

Table of Contents

How To Use This Book

This workbook is designed to help you have a deeper understanding of Dr. McGarey's book. In order to get the most out of the book and apply the concepts, do the following.

1) Read the chapter summary in this book to get an overview and big picture understanding of the book.

2) Read Dr. McGarey's original work. The details of the book will be easier to understand once you grasp the big picture.

3) Once you understand the core concepts, start working through the exercises in this workbook.

4) To assist you with applying the main concepts, the following exercises are present.

Key Takeaways: Main key points to help you understand the most important topics.
Reflective Questions: These questions guide you to reflect on your own experiences and figure out what needs to be done to change your life. Write your thoughts in the lines present in this workbook.
Action Step: Practical steps are discussed to lead you to take action so you can improve your life.

You must **THINK** before doing. This is how you can make changes to lead a new life.

Overview of *The Well-Lived Life: a 102-Year-Old Doctor's Six Secrets to Health and Happiness at Every Age*

"The Well-Lived Life: a 102-Year-Old Doctor's Six Secrets to Health and Happiness at Every Age" is a compelling narrative that encapsulates the wisdom and life lessons of Dr. Gladys McGarey, a pioneer in the field of holistic medicine. The book is a testament to her lifelong journey of learning, growing, and evolving in response to her experiences. It's a guide that encourages readers to approach life with curiosity, extract lessons along the way, and find the courage to face life's challenges.

The book is structured around six secrets or lessons about life, health, and happiness. These secrets, such as "All Life Needs to Move" and "Love Is the Most Powerful Medicine," are presented as chapters that delve into various aspects of living a fulfilling life. Each chapter is a blend of personal anecdotes, professional insights, and practical advice, making the book a rich tapestry of wisdom and inspiration.

Dr. McGarey's work is rooted in the belief that healing comes from within and that love is a powerful medicine. She emphasizes the importance of aligning with life, allowing the energy of love to flow freely into our hearts, and healing our hurts.

In addition to her insights on health and happiness, Dr. McGarey shares her journey, including her pioneering work in integrating allopathic and holistic medical practices. She co-founded the ARE Clinic in Scottsdale,

Arizona, and the Scottsdale Holistic Medical Group, laying the groundwork for the cultural shift towards alternative and holistic medicine modalities.

"The Well-Lived Life" is more than just a book; it's a roadmap to living a fulfilling and meaningful life. It encourages readers to embrace life's lessons, heal their hurts, and spread love to everyone they meet. It's a testament to Dr. McGarey's belief that we live our best lives when we approach life with curiosity and a desire to learn from everything.

Introduction

In the introduction to "The Well-Lived Life," Gladys McGarey, a 102-year-old doctor, invites readers on a journey of self-discovery and personal growth. She presents the book as a guide to finding and activating healing and learning throughout life, to help readers engage fully with every moment. McGarey shares six profound secrets that she believes can help readers face life's challenges and engage with them joyfully and participatory.

The introduction is enriched with personal anecdotes from McGarey's life, including a powerful memory of witnessing Gandhi's Salt March. This experience had a profound impact on her understanding of love and purpose, and she hopes to impart the same unforgettable love to her readers. She emphasizes the importance of connecting with one's truth and soul's purpose and encourages readers to ask deep, burning questions about their identity and purpose in life.

The book includes stories from McGarey's practice and personal life, as well as exercises designed to help readers embody the teachings. She stresses that each reader is ultimately in charge of their healing process and must actively participate in it. The introduction to "The Well-Lived Life" sets the stage for a book that promises to guide readers toward a life of health, happiness, and fulfillment.

Chapter 1: The Juice

Chapter 1 of "The Well-Lived Life," titled "The Juice," introduces readers to the concept of 'juice' as a metaphor for life's energy, purpose, and joy. The chapter begins with a vivid recounting of Gladys McGarey's childhood experience in India, where she assisted her mother in treating a wounded elephant. This event sparked her realization of her calling to be a doctor, despite her struggles with dyslexia.

McGarey introduces the concept of 'juice' as the creative life energy that comes from doing things that matter and mean something to us. It's the energy derived from our unique gifts and purpose in life. She emphasizes that the process of finding our 'juice' keeps us vital and is often more important than the end goal itself.

She notes that losing our 'juice' can be a major obstacle to feeling good and can impact both physical and mental health. She concludes by stating that everyone needs to find their 'juice,' as it's a vital part of our life force. This chapter sets the stage for the exploration of the six secrets to health and happiness that McGarey shares throughout the book.

Key Points

- A childhood experience in India, where McGarey helped her mother treat a wounded elephant, ignited her aspiration to become a doctor.

- 'Juice' is defined as the creative life energy derived from engaging in meaningful activities that align with our unique gifts and life's purpose.

- The journey to discovering our 'juice' is emphasized as a vital process, often holding more significance than the end goal itself.

- The loss of 'juice' can pose a significant challenge to well-being, affecting both physical and mental health.

- The necessity of finding one's 'juice' is underscored, as it constitutes a vital part of our life force.

Milestone Goals

- Reflect on experiences that have given you a sense of purpose and joy. What were you doing? Who were you with?

_____

_____

_____

_____

_____

- Identify activities or pursuits that 'juice' you up. What are you passionate about?

_____

_____

_____

_____

_____

- Consider how you can incorporate more of these 'juice'-giving activities into your daily life.

_____
_____
_____
_____
_____

- Reflect on times when you felt your 'juice' was running out. What were the circumstances? How did you respond?

_____
_____
_____
_____
_____

Action Plan

- Spend some time each day doing something that gives you 'juice.' This could be a hobby, a job, or even a simple daily activity.

_____
_____
_____
_____
_____

- If you're feeling low on 'juice,' take some time to reflect on why this might be. Are there changes you can make to your lifestyle or mindset?

_____

_____

_____

_____

_____

- Seek out new experiences and opportunities that might give you 'juice.' This could involve learning a new skill, starting a new project, or making a change in your career.

_____

_____

_____

_____

_____

- Regularly check in with yourself about your 'juice' levels. If you notice they're running low, take steps to replenish them.

_____

_____

_____

_____

_____

- Share your 'juice' with others. This could involve teaching someone a skill you're passionate about, sharing your experiences, or helping others find their own 'juice.'

_____

_____

_____

Chapter 2: Why Am I Here?

Chapter 2 of "The Well-Lived Life," titled "Why Am I Here?" explores the concept of finding one's 'juice,' or life's purpose and passion. The chapter shares the stories of two individuals, James and Lilian, who are struggling to find their 'juice.'

James, a recent computer science graduate, is unsure about his career path. Despite his degree and the expectations of his parents, he doesn't feel a connection to the field. Through a visualization exercise with McGarey, he realizes his passion for music and decides to pursue a career in music production. This decision fills him with a newfound energy and purpose, his 'juice.'

On the other hand, Lilian, despite having a seemingly perfect life, feels a lack of purpose and meaning. She feels disconnected from her life and believes she has nothing left to live for. McGarey helps Lilian understand that she is part of something bigger and that her life is waiting for her to engage with it. Lilian eventually finds her 'juice' by taking charge of a fundraiser for a children's society from her hospital bed, which revitalizes her and gives her a renewed sense of purpose.

This chapter emphasizes the importance of finding one's 'juice' and how it can transform one's life, providing a sense of purpose, meaning, and vitality.

Key Points

- The journey to finding one's 'juice,' or life's purpose, can be uncertain and challenging, as exemplified by the stories of James and Lilian.

- Career paths aren't always aligned with academic qualifications, as seen in James' shift from computer science to music production.

- Visualization exercises can be instrumental in uncovering hidden passions and redirecting life paths.

- Even amidst perceived perfection, feelings of disconnection and lack of purpose can persist, as experienced by Lilian.

- Engaging with larger causes and community initiatives can help individuals rediscover their 'juice' and regain a sense of purpose.

- The discovery of one's 'juice' can bring about a transformative change, infusing life with renewed energy, purpose, and meaning.

Milestone Goals

- Reflect on your own life. Are there areas where you feel disconnected or lacking in 'juice'?

_____
_____
_____
_____
_____

- Consider your passions and interests. Are there any that you've been neglecting or not pursuing?

_____
_____

_____

_____

_____

- Reflect on the stories of James and Lilian. How do they resonate with your own experiences?

_____

_____

_____

_____

_____

- Think about what gives your life meaning and purpose. What are you passionate about?

_____

_____

_____

_____

_____

Action Plan

- Spend some time each day doing something that gives you 'juice.' This could be a hobby, a job, or even a simple daily activity.

_____

_____

_____

_____

_____

- If you're feeling disconnected or lacking in 'juice,' take some time to reflect on why this might be. Are there changes you can make to your lifestyle or mindset?

- Seek out new experiences and opportunities that might give you 'juice.' This could involve learning a new skill, starting a new project, or making a change in your career.

- Regularly check in with yourself about your 'juice' levels. If you notice they're running low, take steps to replenish them.

- Share your 'juice' with others. This could involve teaching someone a skill you're passionate about, sharing your experiences, or helping others find their own 'juice.'

_____

_____

_____

_____

_____

Chapter 3: Like Pieces of a Jigsaw Puzzle

Chapter 3 of "The Well-Lived Life," titled "Like Pieces of a Jigsaw Puzzle," explores the concept of finding one's unique place and purpose in the world. McGarey likens individuals to pieces of a jigsaw puzzle, each with a unique shape and place in the world. When we find our place in the puzzle, we become part of the pattern of life, and our 'juice' flows freely.

The chapter begins with the story of McGarey's mother, who was inspired to become a doctor after witnessing the transformative power of osteopathic medicine. This story serves as a powerful example of how finding one's 'juice' can lead to a life of purpose and fulfillment.

McGarey shares her struggles with the medical establishment's focus on the disease rather than healing. This led her to develop her unique approach to medicine, which views health challenges as part of our soul's journey and opportunities for growth and learning.

The chapter concludes with a powerful message about the importance of finding and embracing our unique place in the world. By doing so, we can tap into our 'juice,' contribute to the greater whole, and live a life of purpose and fulfillment.

Key Points

- McGarey's mother was inspired to pursue a career in medicine after experiencing the transformative power of osteopathic medicine.

- Individuals are introduced as pieces of a jigsaw puzzle, each possessing a unique shape and place in the world.

- Upon finding our place in the puzzle, we become part of life's pattern, allowing our 'juice' to flow freely.

- Personal struggles with the medical establishment's disease-focused approach led to the development of a unique approach to medicine.

- Health challenges are part of our soul's journey and should be viewed as opportunities for growth and learning.

Milestone Goals

- Reflect on your own 'shape' as a piece of the jigsaw puzzle. What makes you unique? What is your place in the world?

_____
_____
_____
_____
_____

- Consider your health challenges or struggles. How can they be seen as opportunities for growth and learning?

_____
_____
_____

_____

_____

- Reflect on the story of McGarey's mother. How does it resonate with your own experiences?

_____

_____

_____

_____

_____

- Think about your interactions with the medical establishment. How do they align with McGarey's approach to medicine?

_____

_____

_____

_____

_____

Action Plan

- Spend some time each day reflecting on your unique shape and place in the world. This could involve journaling, meditation, or simply quiet contemplation.

_____

_____

_____

_____

_____

- If you're facing health challenges or struggles, consider how they might be opportunities for growth and learning. Seek out resources or support to help you navigate these challenges.

  _____
  _____
  _____
  _____
  _____

- Seek out opportunities to share your 'juice' with the world. This could involve volunteering, mentoring, or simply sharing your experiences and insights with others.

  _____
  _____
  _____
  _____
  _____

- Regularly check in with yourself about your 'juice' levels. If you notice they're running low, take steps to replenish them.

  _____
  _____
  _____
  _____
  _____

- Advocate for a holistic approach to health and healing, both in your interactions with the medical establishment and in your conversations with others.

Chapter 4: Where Should I Pour My Juice?

Chapter 4 of "The Well-Lived Life," titled "Where Should I Pour My Juice?" explores the challenge of deciding where to invest one's energy and passion, or 'juice.' The chapter begins with the story of Anne, a film producer and yoga teacher, who is dealing with recurring bronchitis due to her hectic schedule. Despite her passion for both her jobs, she realizes that she needs to slow down and prioritize her health.

McGarey uses Anne's story to illustrate the importance of balance and self-care in our pursuit of 'juice.' She emphasizes that while it's important to follow our passions, we also need to listen to our bodies and ensure we're not spreading ourselves too thin.

The chapter also discusses the societal pressures to judge our success from the outside, such as whether we're good at something or whether it makes us money or brings us prestige. However, McGarey argues that true happiness comes from how we feel on the inside.

McGarey shares her own experiences of juggling multiple interests and passions, and how they contributed to her 'juice.' She emphasizes that we're complex beings and we're meant to embrace that complexity.

The chapter concludes with a powerful message about the importance of finding balance in our lives. By investing our 'juice' wisely and taking care of ourselves, we can lead more fulfilling and healthier lives.

Key Points

- The story of Anne, a film producer and yoga teacher dealing with recurring bronchitis due to a busy schedule, highlights the need to slow down and prioritize health despite her passion for work.

- Anne's story illustrates the significance of balance and self-care in the pursuit of 'juice.' While following passions is important, it's equally crucial to listen to our bodies and avoid overextending ourselves.

- Societal pressures often push us to measure success externally, such as proficiency in a skill or the money or prestige gains it brings. However, true happiness stems from internal satisfaction.

- Personal experiences of balancing multiple interests and passions contribute to one's 'juice.' It's emphasized that as complex beings, we're meant to embrace this complexity.

Milestone Goals

- Reflect on your own life. Are there areas where you feel you're spreading yourself too thin? Are there passions or interests you're neglecting due to a lack of time or energy?

_____
_____
_____
_____
_____

- Consider your health and well-being. Are you taking enough time for self-care and relaxation?

_____

_____

_____

_____

_____

- Reflect on the story of Anne. How does it resonate
  with your own experiences?

_____

_____

_____

_____

_____

- Think about your passions and interests. Are you
  investing your 'juice' wisely?

_____

_____

_____

_____

_____

Action Plan

- Spend some time each day doing something that
  gives you 'juice.' This could be a hobby, a job, or even
  a simple daily activity.

_____

_____

_____

_____

_____

- If you're feeling overwhelmed or spread too thin, consider where you might be able to cut back or delegate responsibilities.

_____
_____
_____
_____
_____

- Prioritize self-care and relaxation. This could involve taking time each day for relaxation, getting regular exercise, or ensuring you're getting enough sleep.

_____
_____
_____
_____
_____

- Regularly check in with yourself about your 'juice' levels. If you notice they're running low, take steps to replenish them.

_____
_____
_____
_____
_____

- Seek out new experiences and opportunities that might give you 'juice.' This could involve learning a new skill, starting a new project, or making a change in your career.

Chapter 5: Connecting with Desire

Chapter 5 of "The Well-Lived Life," titled "Connecting with Desire," explores the importance of recognizing and pursuing what one truly desires in life, which McGarey refers to as one's 'juice.' The chapter begins by discussing the fear and uncertainty that often accompanies the process of identifying one's desires. McGarey encourages readers to allow themselves to want and yearn for things, arguing that this is a natural part of life.

McGarey shares her own experiences of struggling with desire and the fear of wanting too much or wanting things that seem unattainable. She emphasizes the importance of listening to one's heart and following its guidance. The chapter includes practice for finding one's 'juice,' which involves reflecting on times when one felt a sense of purpose and joy, and identifying what brings one joy in the present.

McGarey suggests that once one has identified their 'juice,' they should seek out ways to incorporate it into their daily life. This could involve taking on a new project, helping others, or simply doing something that brings joy. The chapter concludes with the message that the search for one's 'juice' is as important as finding it. The process of searching is a form of life reaching for life, and even the longing for more 'juice' is a sign of one's potential for growth and fulfillment.

Key Points

- Fear and uncertainty often accompany the process of identifying one's desires. It's encouraged to allow oneself to want and yearn for things, as this is a natural aspect of life.

- Personal experiences of struggling with desire and the fear of wanting too much or desiring seemingly unattainable things highlight the importance of listening to one's heart and following its guidance.

- A practice for finding one's 'juice' involves reflecting on instances of feeling a sense of purpose and joy, and identifying what brings joy in the present.

- Once one's 'juice' is identified, seek ways to incorporate it into daily life. This could involve initiating a new project, assisting others, or simply engaging in activities that bring joy.

- The pursuit of one's 'juice' is as significant as its discovery. The process of searching is a form of life reaching for life, and even the longing for more 'juice' signifies one's potential for growth and fulfillment.

Milestone Goals

- Reflect on your desires. What do you truly want in life? What brings you joy and fulfillment?

_____

_____

_____

_____

_____

- Consider any fears or uncertainties you have about pursuing your desires. How can you address these fears and move forward?

_____

_____

_____

_____

_____

- Reflect on the practice for finding your 'juice.' How can you incorporate this practice into your daily life?

_____

_____

_____

_____

_____

- Think about how you can incorporate more of your 'juice' into your daily life. What changes can you make to pursue your desires more fully?

_____

_____

_____

_____

_____

Action Plan

- Spend some time each day reflecting on your desires and what brings you joy. This could involve journaling, meditation, or simply quiet contemplation.

_____
_____
_____
_____
_____
_____

- If you're feeling uncertain or fearful about pursuing your desires, consider seeking support from a trusted friend, family member, or counselor.

_____
_____
_____
_____
_____

- Incorporate more of your 'juice' into your daily life. This could involve taking on a new project, helping others, or simply doing something that brings you joy.

_____
_____
_____
_____
_____

- Regularly check in with yourself about your 'juice' levels. If you notice they're running low, take steps to replenish them.

_____
_____
_____

_____

_____

- Remember that the search for your 'juice' is as important as finding it. Embrace the process of searching and see it as a form of growth and self-discovery.

_____

_____

_____

_____

_____

Secret II: All Life Needs to Move
Chapter 6: Feeling Stuck

Chapter 6 of "The Well-Lived Life," titled "Feeling Stuck," explores the experience of feeling unable to move forward in life, and how this can manifest both physically and emotionally. The chapter begins by discussing the common experience of feeling 'stuck' in life, whether due to trauma, heartbreak, or a lack of motivation or passion.

McGarey shares the story of a patient named Theresa, who was suffering from severe intestinal obstructions. Despite trying everything she knew to do physically, the blockages persisted. Through her discussions with Theresa, McGarey uncovers a connection between Theresa's physical blockages and her emotional state, particularly her experience of multiple losses.

The chapter introduces the concept of anicca or anitya, an ancient Buddhist and Hindu concept that focuses on the impermanence of life and the suffering that comes when we try to stop its flow. McGarey suggests that understanding the power of movement can help us get through almost anything, whether we're feeling stuck physically, emotionally, or spiritually.

The chapter concludes with the message that even when we feel stuck, life itself is always moving. By embracing this movement and the impermanence of life, we can navigate through our hardest moments and find our 'juice' again.

Key Points

- The feeling of being 'stuck' in life, whether due to trauma, heartbreak, or a lack of motivation or passion, is a common experience.

- The story of a patient named Theresa, suffering from severe intestinal obstructions, illustrates that despite physical efforts, blockages can persist.

- There is a connection between our physical, emotional, and mental states, and issues in one area can influence others. For instance, Theresa's physical blockages were tied to her emotional state and her experience of loss.

- The concept of anicca or anitya, an ancient Buddhist and Hindu concept emphasizing the impermanence of life and the suffering that arises when we attempt to halt its flow, is introduced.

- Understanding the power of movement can aid in navigating through almost anything, applicable at the physical, emotional, and spiritual levels.

Milestone Goals

- Reflect on your own life. Are there areas where you feel 'stuck'? What might be causing this feeling?

_____
_____
_____
_____
_____

- Consider your physical health. Are there any issues that might be linked to your emotional or mental state?

  _____

  _____

  _____

  _____

  _____

- Reflect on the concept of anicca or anitya. How does this concept resonate with your own experiences?

  _____

  _____

  _____

  _____

  _____

- Think about how you can incorporate more movement into your life, both physically and emotionally.

  _____

  _____

  _____

  _____

  _____

Action Plan

- Spend some time each day reflecting on areas where you feel 'stuck.' This could involve journaling, meditation, or simply quiet contemplation.

_____

_____

_____

_____

_____

_____

- If you're experiencing physical health issues, consider whether they might be linked to your emotional or mental state. Seek support from a healthcare professional if needed.

_____

_____

_____

_____

_____

- Incorporate more movement into your life. This could involve physical exercise, but also emotional 'movement' such as expressing your feelings or seeking support for mental health issues.

_____

_____

_____

_____

_____

- Regularly check in with yourself about your 'juice' levels. If you notice they're running low, take steps to replenish them.

_____

_____

_____

_____

_____

- Embrace the concept of anicca or anitya in your daily
  life. Try to accept the impermanence of life and the
  flow of experiences, rather than resisting them.

_____

_____

_____

_____

_____

Chapter 7: Life is Always Moving

Chapter 7 of "The Well-Lived Life," titled "Life is Always Moving," delves into the concept of movement as a fundamental aspect of life and how feeling 'stuck' can be a barrier to this natural flow. McGarey uses the metaphor of a forest stream to illustrate the idea that life is always moving, even when it seems stagnant or stuck.

McGarey shares her experiences with acupuncture and how it helped her understand the concept of energy flow in the body. She discusses how acupuncture can help unblock energy channels and restore movement, providing an example of a patient who experienced relief from labor pain through acupuncture.

The chapter emphasizes the importance of physical movement for overall health and well-being. McGarey shares her practice of walking and how it helps her maintain her energy levels. She also introduces the concept of meridians, energy channels in the body that are a fundamental part of traditional Chinese medicine.

The chapter concludes with the message that embracing the concept of life as a movement can help us overcome feelings of being stuck and reconnect with our 'juice.' By recognizing and aligning with the natural flow of life, we can navigate through our hardest moments and find our 'juice' again.

Key Points

- Life is perceived as a continuous movement, even in instances of perceived stagnation or blockage. This idea is illustrated through the metaphor of a forest stream.

- Experiences with acupuncture have contributed to understanding the concept of energy flow within the body. Acupuncture can aid in unblocking energy channels and reinstating movement.

- Physical movement holds significant importance for overall health and well-being. Personal practices, such as walking, can help maintain energy levels.

- The concept of meridians, energy channels within the body that are integral to traditional Chinese medicine, is introduced. Treatments like acupuncture can assist in unblocking these meridians and restoring energy flow.

- Embracing the concept of life as a movement can aid in overcoming feelings of stagnation and reestablishing a connection with our 'juice.'

Milestone Goals

- Reflect on your own life. Are there areas where you feel 'stuck'? What might be causing this feeling?

_____

_____

_____

_____

_____

- Consider your physical health. Are there any issues that might be linked to your emotional or mental state?

_____

_____

_____

_____

_____

- Reflect on the concept of life as a movement. How does this concept resonate with your own experiences?

_____

_____

_____

_____

_____

- Think about how you can incorporate more movement into your life, both physically and emotionally.

_____

_____

_____

_____

_____

Action Plan

- Spend some time each day moving your body. This could involve walking, dancing, yoga, or any other form of physical exercise that you enjoy.

_____
_____
_____
_____
_____

- If you're feeling 'stuck' in any area of your life, consider seeking support from a healthcare professional, counselor, or trusted friend.

_____
_____
_____
_____
_____

- Incorporate practices that promote energy flow into your daily routine. This could involve practices like yoga, tai chi, or even acupuncture.

_____
_____
_____
_____
_____

- Regularly check in with yourself about your 'juice' levels. If you notice they're running low, take steps to replenish them.

_____
_____
_____
_____
_____

- Embrace the concept of life as a movement in your daily life. Try to see the movement and change in all aspects of your life, even when things seem stagnant or stuck.

Chapter 8 of "The Well-Lived Life," titled "Moving Through Pain," discusses the concept of movement as a way to navigate through physical and emotional pain. The chapter begins with the story of Maria, a young mother suffering from headaches and depression. McGarey uses Maria's story to illustrate the paralyzing effect of pain and depression, and how even small movements can help alleviate these conditions.

McGarey discusses the importance of movement in overcoming pain and depression. She suggests that even small movements, like deepening one's breathing or moving in rhythm with a child, can help alleviate pain and improve mood. She introduces the concept of fear as a barrier to movement, arguing that fear of exacerbating pain often leads people to avoid movement, which can worsen their condition.

The chapter includes examples of patients suffering from chronic pain and depression, and how encouraging them to move helped improve their conditions. McGarey emphasizes that movement is a powerful tool for navigating through pain and depression. By embracing movement, we can overcome our fears and reconnect with our 'juice.' The chapter concludes with the message that even when we're in pain, life itself is always moving, and by aligning with this movement, we can navigate through our hardest moments and find our 'juice' again.

Key Points

- Movement plays a crucial role in combating pain and depression. Even minor movements, such as deepening one's breathing or moving in sync with a child, can alleviate pain and enhance mood.

- Fear is identified as an obstacle to movement. The fear of intensifying pain often discourages people from moving, which can paradoxically worsen their condition.

- Experiences with patients suffering from chronic pain and depression demonstrate that encouraging movement can significantly improve their conditions.

- Movement is a potent tool for managing pain and depression. By embracing movement, individuals can overcome their fears and reestablish their connection with their 'juice.'

Milestone Goals

- Reflect on your own experiences with pain and depression. How have these experiences affected your movement and energy levels?

_____
_____
_____⟩_____
_____
_____

- Consider your physical health. Are there any issues that might be linked to your emotional or mental state?

_____
_____

_____

_____

_____

- Reflect on the concept of movement as a way to navigate through pain. How does this concept resonate with your own experiences?

_____

_____

_____

_____

_____

- Think about how you can incorporate more movement into your life, both physically and emotionally.

_____

_____

_____

_____

_____

Action Plan

- Spend some time each day moving your body. This could involve walking, dancing, yoga, or any other form of physical exercise that you enjoy.

_____

_____

_____

_____

_____

- If you're experiencing pain or depression, consider seeking support from a healthcare professional, counselor, or trusted friend.

_____

_____

_____

_____

_____

- Incorporate practices that promote movement into your daily routine. This could involve practices like yoga, tai chi, or even simple breathing exercises.

_____

_____

_____

_____

_____

- Regularly check in with yourself about your 'juice' levels. If you notice they're running low, take steps to replenish them.

_____

_____

_____

_____

_____

- Embrace the concept of movement in your daily life. Try to see the movement and change in all aspects of your life, even when things seem stagnant or stuck.

Chapter 9: Locked in Shame

Chapter 9 of "The Well-Lived Life," titled "Locked in Shame," discusses the concept of shame as a paralyzing emotion and how movement and humor can help release it. McGarey begins the chapter by asserting that shame is one of the hardest emotions to release, often causing people to live their lives in its grip.

She shares personal anecdotes of embarrassing moments, such as slipping and falling onstage, to illustrate how shame can be transformed into humor. She discusses the importance of self-forgiveness in releasing shame and regret, especially regarding past decisions and mistakes.

McGarey introduces the concept of laughter as a physical movement that can help release shame. She explains how laughter physically affects the body, particularly the adrenal glands, and can help alleviate stress and upset. She shares a humorous incident from her 99th birthday to illustrate this concept.

The chapter concludes with the message that releasing shame and embracing humor and movement can help us reconnect with our 'juice.' By recognizing and aligning with the natural flow of life, we can navigate through our hardest moments and find our 'juice' again.

Key Points

- Shame is one of the most difficult emotions to let go of, often leading individuals to live under its influence.

- Personal experiences of embarrassing incidents, such as slipping and falling onstage, can transform shame into humor.

- Self-forgiveness plays a significant role in releasing shame and regret, especially when it comes to prior decisions and mistakes.

- Laughter, as a physical activity, aids in the release of shame. It has a physical impact on the body, specifically the adrenal glands, and can help mitigate stress and distress.

- Releasing shame and adopting humor and movement can aid in reestablishing our connection with our 'juice.'

Milestone Goals

- Reflect on your own experiences with shame. How have these experiences affected your movement and energy levels?

_____

_____

_____

_____

_____

- Consider how humor might help you release feelings of shame or embarrassment.

_____

_____

_____

_____

_____

- Reflect on past decisions or mistakes that you regret. How can self-forgiveness help you release these feelings?

_____

_____

_____

_____

_____

- Think about how you can incorporate more movement and laughter into your life.

_____

_____

_____

_____

_____

Action Plan

- Spend some time each day reflecting on areas where you feel shame. This could involve journaling, meditation, or simply quiet contemplation.

_____

_____

_____

_____

_____

- If you're feeling shame or embarrassment, consider seeking support from a counselor or trusted friend.

_____

_____

_____

_____

_____

- Incorporate more laughter into your daily life. This could involve watching a funny movie, spending time with friends who make you laugh, or even practicing laughter yoga.

_____

_____

_____

_____

_____

- Regularly check in with yourself about your 'juice' levels. If you notice they're running low, take steps to replenish them.

_____

_____

_____

_____

_____

- Embrace the concept of movement in your daily life. Try to see the movement and change in all aspects of your life, even when things seem stagnant or stuck.

Chapter 10: Releasing What Doesn't Matter

Chapter 10 of "The Well-Lived Life," titled "Releasing What Doesn't Matter," discusses the concept of letting go of regrets, mistakes, and past experiences that no longer serve us. McGarey begins the chapter by acknowledging that many people struggle with feeling stuck on an idea or experience, and sometimes we can't manage to move on.

She shares a personal anecdote about a young father who nearly killed his newborn baby by accident. She uses this story to illustrate the importance of forgiving ourselves for past mistakes and emphasizes that most people did the best they could with the information they had at the time.

McGarey introduces the concept of "Kutch par wa nay," a phrase in Hindustani meaning "It doesn't matter." She explains how this phrase can be used to let go of things that no longer serve us. She shares how her mother used this phrase and gesture to let go of things that didn't serve her, and how she has adopted this practice in her own life.

The chapter concludes with the message that letting go of what doesn't matter and focusing on what does can help us reconnect with our 'juice.' By recognizing and aligning with the natural flow of life, we can navigate through our hardest moments and find our 'juice' again.

Key Points

- Many people struggle with feeling stuck on an idea or experience, and sometimes we can't manage to move on.

- It's important to forgive ourselves for past mistakes.

- It's important to release regret and move on.

- "Kutch par wa nay," is a phrase in Hindustani meaning "It doesn't matter." This phrase can be used to let go of things that no longer serve us.

- Letting go of what doesn't matter and focusing on what does can help us reconnect with our 'juice.'

Milestone Goals

- Reflect on your own experiences with regret. How have these experiences affected your movement and energy levels?

- Consider how the phrase "Kutch par wa nay" might help you release feelings of regret or past mistakes.

- Reflect on past decisions or mistakes that you regret. How can self-forgiveness help you release these feelings?

_____

_____

_____

- Think about how you can incorporate the concept of "Kutch par wa nay" into your life.

_____

_____

_____

_____

_____

Action Plan

- Spend some time each day reflecting on areas where you feel regret. This could involve journaling, meditation, or simply quiet contemplation.

_____

_____

_____

_____

_____

- If you're feeling regretful or stuck on an experience, consider seeking support from a counselor or trusted friend.

_____

_____

_____

_____

_____

- Incorporate the phrase "Kutch par wa nay" into your daily life. Use it as a mantra to help you let go of things that no longer serve you.

- Regularly check in with yourself about your 'juice' levels. If you notice they're running low, take steps to replenish them.

- Embrace the concept of movement in your daily life. Try to see the movement and change in all aspects of your life, even when things seem stagnant or stuck.

Chapter 11: Removing the Blockage

Chapter 11 of "The Well-Lived Life" discusses the concept of removing blockages in life and health. Dr. McGarey uses the story of her patient, Shanti, to illustrate this concept. Shanti was pregnant and determined to have an intervention-free birth. However, she was resistant to the physical exercises prescribed by Dr. McGarey and the nurse midwife, Barbara Brown. This resistance manifested as a physical blockage during labor, with Shanti's cervix not dilating as it should. Barbara found a way around this blockage by tapping into Shanti's spiritual practice of chanting, which eventually led to the successful birth of a healthy baby.

Dr. McGarey also shares the story of her friend and colleague, Elisabeth Kübler-Ross, who faced a significant blockage in her life. Elisabeth faced hostility from her community in Virginia due to her progressive ideas and her work with AIDS patients. After her home was burglarized and set on fire, Elisabeth decided to move to Scottsdale, Arizona. This move represented the removal of a major blockage in her life, allowing her to continue her work in a more supportive community.

Key Points

- Removing blockages, whether physical, mental, or situational, can lead to significant progress and healing.

- Sometimes, the key to removing a blockage lies in tapping into a different aspect of our lives, as seen in Shanti's story.

- Major life decisions, such as Elisabeth's decision to move, can represent the removal of a blockage.

- Focusing on what we want can help us understand what is and isn't working in our lives, aiding in the removal of blockages.

Milestone Goals

- What blockages are you currently facing in your life? How are they affecting you?

_____

_____

_____

_____

_____

- How can you tap into different aspects of your life to work around these blockages?

_____

_____

_____

_____

_____

- Are there any major life decisions you need to make to remove a blockage?

_____

_____

_____

_____

_____

- How can focusing on what you want help you identify and remove blockages?

_____

_____

_____

_____

_____

Action Plan

- Identify any blockages you are currently facing in your life.

_____

_____

_____

_____

_____

- Consider how you can tap into different aspects of your life to work around these blockages.

_____

_____

_____

_____

_____

- If necessary, make any major life decisions needed to remove a blockage.

_____

_____

_____

_____

_____

- Focus on what you want in life to help you identify
  and remove blockages.

_____

_____

_____

_____

_____

Chapter 12: Look for the Trickle Around the Dam

Chapter 12 of "The Well-Lived Life," titled "Look for the Trickle Around the Dam," discusses the concept of finding the small signs of life's natural movement even when we feel stuck. McGarey begins the chapter by asserting that life is always moving, and even when we feel stuck, there's always a trickle forming around the dam.

She shares a personal anecdote about a patient named Theresa who suffered from intestinal obstruction. After experiencing an emotional shift after releasing her sadness, having sobbed when McGarey inquired as to her grieving process, Theresa's obstruction dissipated. McGarey uses this story to illustrate the importance of allowing our emotions to move, and how this can have a profound impact on our physical health.

The chapter points to the importance of letting our grief move. McGarey suggests that grief isn't quite the same as depression—grief moves, while depression stands still. She introduces the concept of focusing on our love for whomever or whatever was lost while letting the suffering pass through us.

The chapter concludes with a practice for letting go. McGarey provides a step-by-step guide for physical exercise that can help release feelings of stuckness. By recognizing and aligning with the natural flow of life, we can navigate through our hardest moments and find our 'juice' again.

Key Points

- Life is always moving, and even when we feel stuck, there's always a trickle forming around the dam.

- It's important to allow our emotions to move.

- It's also important to let our grief move. Grief isn't quite the same as depression—grief moves, while depression stands still.

- Focusing on our love for whomever or whatever was lost, while letting the suffering pass through us, can help us heal.

Milestone Goals

- Reflect on your own experiences with feeling stuck. How have these experiences affected your movement and energy levels?

_____
_____
_____
_____
_____

- Consider how the concept of the "trickle around the dam" might help you release feelings of stuckness.

_____
_____
_____
_____
_____

- Reflect on your experiences with grief. How can allowing your grief to move help you release these feelings?

_____

_____

_____

_____

_____

- Think about how you can incorporate the practice of letting go into your life.

_____

_____

_____

_____

_____

Action Plan

- Spend some time each day reflecting on areas where you feel stuck. This could involve journaling, meditation, or simply quiet contemplation.

_____

_____

_____

_____

_____

- If you're feeling stuck or grieving, consider seeking support from a counselor or trusted friend.

_____

_____

_____

_____

_____

- Incorporate the practice of letting go into your daily
  life. Follow the steps provided in the chapter to help
  you release feelings of stuckness.

_____

_____

_____

_____

_____

- Regularly check in with yourself about your 'juice'
  levels. If you notice they're running low, take steps to
  replenish them.

_____

_____

_____

_____

_____

- Embrace the concept of movement in your daily life.
  Try to see the movement and change in all aspects of
  your life, even when things seem stagnant or stuck.

_____

_____

_____

_____

_____

Secret III: Love Is the Most Powerful Medicine

Chapter 13: Love and Fear

Chapter 13 of "The Well-Lived Life," titled "Love and Fear," discusses the relationship between these two powerful emotions and how choosing love can lead to healing and growth. McGarey begins the chapter with a story of Susan, a young teacher who was in a terrible car accident and was told she would never walk again. This story illustrates the power of fear and how it can paralyze us.

McGarey emphasizes the importance of acknowledging fear but not letting it control us. She suggests that fear can block love, which is a powerful healing force. She discusses the transformative power of love, asserting that love can change everything it touches, making labor blissful, laughter joyful, and listening meaningful.

McGarey introduces the concept of choosing love over fear. She suggests that we have a choice in every moment to focus on love or fear, and choosing love can lead to healing and growth. The chapter concludes with the message that love is the most powerful medicine. Our life force is activated by love. By recognizing and aligning with the power of love, we can navigate through our hardest moments and find our 'juice' again.

Key Points

- Fear can be powerful, and it can paralyze us.

- It's important to acknowledge fear but not let it control us. Fear can block love, which is a powerful healing force.

- Love has transformative power. Love can change everything it touches, making labor blissful, laughter joyful, and listening meaningful.

- We have a choice in every moment to focus on love or fear, and choosing love can lead to healing and growth.

- Love is the most powerful medicine. Our life force is activated by love.

Milestone Goals

- Reflect on your own experiences with fear and love. How have these experiences affected your life?

_____

_____

_____

_____

_____

- Consider how choosing love over fear might change your perspective and lead to growth.

_____

_____

_____

_____

_____

- Reflect on your experiences with healing. How can love contribute to this process?

  _____
  _____
  _____
  _____
  _____

- Think about how you can incorporate the practice of choosing love over fear into your life.

  _____
  _____
  _____
  _____
  _____

Action Plan

- Spend some time each day reflecting on your emotions. This could involve journaling, meditation, or simply quiet contemplation.

  _____
  _____
  _____
  _____
  _____

- If you're feeling fear, consider seeking support from a counselor or trusted friend.

  _____
  _____

_____

_____

_____

- Practice choosing love over fear in your daily life.
  Notice how this choice affects your emotions and
  experiences.

_____

_____

_____

_____

_____

- Regularly check in with yourself about your 'juice'
  levels. If you notice they're running low, take steps to
  replenish them.

_____

_____

_____

_____

_____

- Embrace the concept of love in your daily life. Try to
  see the love in all aspects of your life, even when
  things seem challenging or fearful.

_____

_____

_____

_____

_____

Chapter 14: Choice

Chapter 14 of "The Well-Lived Life," titled "Choice," discusses the power of choice and how it can be used to navigate through life's challenges. McGarey begins the chapter by asserting that there's always something we can do, even when we face our greatest challenges. This doesn't mean that the bad things that happen are our fault, but rather that we have an opportunity to choose what we do and how we respond.

She shares the story of Dr. Elisabeth Kübler-Ross, who chose love over fear, anger, and pain after being victimized by a crime. This story illustrates the power of choice in healing and moving forward.

The chapter also discusses the role of the unconscious mind in our choices and behaviors. McGarey introduces the work of psychologist and psychotherapist Milton Erickson, who believed that changes in the unconscious could affect a patient's day-to-day life. She emphasizes the importance of directing our intention toward our unconscious beliefs and the often painful events that have contributed to them, suggesting that nearly anything that happened in the past can be healed.

The chapter concludes with the message that choice is our first act of self-love, and all love is based on self-love. By recognizing and aligning with the power of choice, we can navigate through our hardest moments and find our 'juice' again.

Key Points

- There's always something we can do, even when we face our greatest challenges. This doesn't mean that the bad things that happen are our fault, but rather that we have an opportunity to choose what we do and how we respond.

- The unconscious mind plays a significant role in our choices and behaviors. McGarey introduces the work of psychologist and psychotherapist Milton Erickson, who believed that changes in the unconscious could affect a patient's day-to-day life.

- It's important to direct our intention toward our unconscious beliefs and the often painful events that have contributed to them. Nearly anything that happened in the past can be healed.

- Choice is our first act of self-love, and all love is based on self-love.

Milestone Goals

- Reflect on your own experiences with choice. How have these experiences affected your life?

_____
_____
_____
_____
_____

- Consider how the power of choice might change your perspective and lead to growth.

_____

_____

_____

_____

_____

_____

- Reflect on your experiences with healing. How can choice contribute to this process?

_____

_____

_____

_____

_____

- Think about how you can incorporate the practice of making conscious choices into your life.

_____

_____

_____

_____

_____

Action Plan

- Spend some time each day reflecting on your choices. This could involve journaling, meditation, or simply quiet contemplation.

_____

_____

_____

_____

_____

- If you're feeling stuck or facing a challenge, consider seeking support from a counselor or trusted friend.

_____
_____
_____
_____
_____

- Practice making conscious choices in your daily life. Notice how these choices affect your emotions and experiences.

_____
_____
_____
_____
_____

- Regularly check in with yourself about your 'juice' levels. If you notice they're running low, take steps to replenish them.

_____
_____
_____
_____
_____

- Embrace the concept of choice in your daily life. Try to see the power of choice in all aspects of your life, even when things seem challenging or fearful.

_____
_____

Chapter 15: The Role of Self-Love

Chapter 15 of "The Well-Lived Life," titled "The Role of Self-Love," discusses the importance of self-love in the healing process and how it forms the basis for all other forms of love. McGarey begins the chapter by asserting that self-love is crucial for our well-being and forms the basis for all the love we give and receive.

McGarey shares her personal experiences with cancer: breast cancer, and thyroid cancer. She used visualization and self-love to aid her healing process in both instances. She believes that her mindset and thoughts surrounding her treatments were just as important as the treatments themselves.

The chapter concludes with the message that self-love is the basis of all love—all the love we give and all the love we receive. By recognizing and aligning with the power of self-love, we can navigate through our hardest moments and find our 'juice' again.

Key Points

- Self-love is crucial for our well-being and forms the basis for all the love we give and receive.

- Our mindset toward the treatment of physical ailments can be just as important as the treatment methodologies themselves.

Milestone Goals

- Reflect on your own experiences with self-love. How have these experiences affected your life?

_____
_____
_____
_____
_____
_____

- Consider how the power of self-love might change your perspective and lead to growth.

_____
_____
_____
_____
_____

- Reflect on your experiences with healing. How can self-love contribute to this process?

_____
_____
_____
_____
_____

- Think about how you can incorporate the practice of self-love into your life.

_____
_____
_____
_____
_____

Action Plan

- Spend some time each day reflecting on your self-love. This could involve journaling, meditation, or simply quiet contemplation.

_____

_____

_____

_____

_____

- If you're feeling unloved or facing a challenge, consider seeking support from a counselor or trusted friend.

_____

_____

_____

_____

_____

- Practice self-love in your daily life. Notice how this practice affects your emotions and experiences.

_____

_____

_____

_____

_____

- Regularly check in with yourself about your 'juice' levels. If you notice they're running low, take steps to replenish them.

_____

_____

_____

_____

_____

● Embrace the concept of self-love in your daily life.
   Try to see the power of self-love in all aspects of your
   life, even when things seem challenging or fearful.

_____

_____

_____

_____

_____

Chapter 16: How to Let Love In

Chapter 16 of "The Well-Lived Life," titled "How to Let Love In," discusses the importance of self-love and the ability to receive love from others as a crucial part of healing and personal growth. McGarey begins the chapter with the story of Pamela, a patient who struggled with self-esteem and self-love due to a painful past. This story illustrates the impact of our beliefs about ourselves on our health and happiness. McGarey emphasizes the importance of acknowledging our worthiness of love and the necessity of healing past hurts to let love in.

She suggests that animals can often be a source of unconditional love that helps people begin to let love in, especially when it's hard to receive love from humans. The chapter concludes with the message that health and happiness will follow once we're able to receive love, and the natural response is to spread love to everyone we meet. By recognizing and aligning with the power of love, we can navigate through our hardest moments and find our 'juice' again.

Key Points

- Our beliefs about ourselves are linked to our health and happiness.

- To let love in, it's important to acknowledge our worthiness of love and the necessity of healing past hurts.

- Animals can often be a source of unconditional love that helps people begin to let love in, especially when it's hard to receive love from humans.

- Once we're able to receive love, health and happiness will follow, and the natural response is to spread love to everyone we meet.

Milestone Goals

- Reflect on your own experiences with self-love and receiving love from others. How have these experiences affected your life?

_____
_____
_____
_____
_____

- Consider how the ability to let love in might change your perspective and lead to growth.

_____
_____
_____
_____
_____

- Reflect on your experiences with healing. How can self-love and the ability to receive love contribute to this process?

_____
_____
_____
_____
_____

- Think about how you can incorporate the practice of self-love and letting love into your life.

_____

_____

_____

_____

_____

Action Plan

- Spend some time each day reflecting on your self-love and your ability to receive love. This could involve journaling, meditation, or simply quiet contemplation.

_____

_____

_____

_____

_____

- If you're feeling unloved or facing a challenge, consider seeking support from a counselor or trusted friend.

_____

_____

_____

_____

_____

- Practice self-love and letting love in your daily life. Notice how this practice affects your emotions and experiences.

_____

_____

_____

_____

_____

- Regularly check in with yourself about your 'juice' levels. If you notice they're running low, take steps to replenish them.

_____

_____

_____

_____

_____

- Embrace the concept of self-love and let love in your daily life. Try to see the power of love in all aspects of your life, even when things seem challenging or fearful.

_____

_____

_____

_____

_____

Chapter 17: Giving Love to Others

Chapter 17 of "The Well-Lived Life," titled "Giving Love to Others," discusses the importance of giving love to others as a crucial part of healing, personal growth, and overall well-being. McGarey begins the chapter with her childhood experiences of receiving love from her parents, who were devout Presbyterians and believed in healing through the power of love.

She shares her parents' commitment to love and healing, emphasizing that their faith was rightfully used, as the basis of their commitment was love. The chapter discusses the role of love in healing and personal growth. McGarey suggests that if she can't love someone, she considers it her problem, not the other person's, and she finds a way to love them anyway.

She emphasizes the importance of letting love flow into and out of the heart freely, without stopping it. She views loving as a key part of our health and well-being. The chapter concludes with the message that even when we understand the importance of love, life can throw us unexpected challenges that can lead to fear. However, once love flows both into and out of our hearts, we can resist the temptation to fall back into fear. By recognizing and aligning with the power of love, we can navigate through our hardest moments and find our 'juice' again.

Key Points

- Love is essential to healing and personal growth. McGarey suggests that if she can't love someone, she considers it her problem, not the other person's, and she finds a way to love them anyway.

- It is important to let love flow into and out of the heart freely, without stopping it. Loving is a key part of our health and well-being.

- Even when we understand the importance of love, life can throw us unexpected challenges that can lead to fear. Using love can help us keep fear at bay.

Milestone Goals

- Reflect on your own experiences with giving and receiving love. How have these experiences affected your life?

_____
_____
_____
_____
_____

- Consider how the power of giving love to others might change your perspective and lead to growth.

_____
_____
_____
_____
_____

- Reflect on your experiences with healing. How can giving love to others contribute to this process?

_____
_____
_____

_____
_____

- Think about how you can incorporate the practice of giving love to others into your life.

_____
_____
_____
_____
_____

Action Plan

- Spend some time each day reflecting on your love for others. This could involve journaling, meditation, or simply quiet contemplation.

_____
_____
_____
_____
_____

- If you're feeling unloved or facing a challenge, consider seeking support from a counselor or trusted friend.

_____
_____
_____
_____
_____

- Practice giving love to others in your daily life. Notice how this practice affects your emotions and experiences.

  _____

  _____

  _____

  _____

  _____

- Regularly check in with yourself about your 'juice' levels. If you notice they're running low, take steps to replenish them.

  _____

  _____

  _____

  _____

  _____

- Embrace the concept of giving love to others in your daily life. Try to see the power of love in all aspects of your life, even when things seem challenging or fearful.

  _____

  _____

  _____

  _____

  _____

Chapter 18: Love and Miracles

Chapter 18 of "The Well-Lived Life," titled "Love and Miracles," discusses the transformative power of love, even in the face of adversity and fear. McGarey begins the chapter with the story of Carolyn, a patient who had suffered five miscarriages and was on the verge of losing her sixth pregnancy. McGarey advised her to communicate her love to her unborn child, which resulted in the successful birth of a healthy baby. Shockingly, a scar at birth indicated that a cleft lip and palate had healed on its own. The stage of soft palate formation coincided with when the patient communicated with her child.

McGarey emphasizes the importance of love as a healing force, even when faced with fear and uncertainty. She suggests that love can lead to miraculous outcomes, as seen in Carolyn's story. The chapter discusses the role of love in personal growth and healing. McGarey suggests that love can help us navigate through dark times and unexpected challenges.

She emphasizes the importance of self-love and the nourishment it provides to our cells. She suggests that we don't need to wait until we're suffering to start offering ourselves love as medicine. The chapter concludes with the message that love can create miracles, both big and small. By choosing love over fear, we can experience increased meaning and happiness in our lives.

Key Points

- Love serves as a vital healing force when one is faced with fear and uncertainty.

- Love can help us navigate through dark times and unexpected challenges.

- Self-love provides nourishment to our cells. We don't need to wait until we're suffering to start offering ourselves love as medicine.

- Love can create miracles, both big and small. By choosing love over fear, we can experience increased meaning and happiness in our lives.

Milestone Goals

- Reflect on your own experiences with love and miracles. How have these experiences affected your life?

_____
_____
_____
_____
_____

- Consider how the power of love might change your perspective and lead to growth.

_____
_____
_____
_____
_____

- Reflect on your experiences with healing. How can love contribute to this process?

_____

_____

_____

_____

_____

- Think about how you can incorporate the practice of love into your life.

_____

_____

_____

_____

_____

Action Plan

- Spend some time each day reflecting on your experiences with love. This could involve journaling, meditation, or simply quiet contemplation.

_____

_____

_____

_____

_____

- If you're facing a challenge, consider seeking support from a counselor or trusted friend.

_____

_____

_____

_____

_____

- Practice love in your daily life. Notice how this practice affects your emotions and experiences.

_____

_____

_____

_____

_____

- Regularly check in with yourself about your 'juice' levels. If you notice they're running low, take steps to replenish them.

_____

_____

_____

_____

_____

- Embrace the concept of love in your daily life. Try to see the power of love in all aspects of your life, even when things seem challenging or fearful.

_____

_____

_____

_____

_____

Chapter 19 of "The Well-Lived Life," titled "Life is Connection," emphasizes the importance of community and connection in our lives. McGarey begins the chapter with her fond memories of her childhood winter field camps, where everyone had a job to do and the work was joyful. She loved the sense of connection and community.

She shares the story of Sadhu Sundar Singh, a Christian convert who believed in spreading his faith by acting as Jesus did while remaining fully Indian. His presence facilitated connection, something McGarey admired and wanted to emulate. The chapter discusses the role of connection in personal growth and healing. McGarey suggests that we thrive when we receive others' attempts to connect with us and when we offer connection to others.

She emphasizes the importance of community, even in the face of great struggles. She shares her vision of a Village for Living Medicine, where healing, living, and learning are combined. The chapter concludes with the message that despite the increasing ideological divisions in society, we are social beings meant to be together. This is how we thrive. By recognizing and aligning with the power of connection, we can navigate through our hardest moments and find our 'juice' again.

Key Points

- When we receive others' attempts to connect with us and when we offer connection to others, we can contribute to our personal growth and healing.

- When faced with great struggles, a community can act as a compass in helping us navigate hardship.

- Despite the increasing ideological divisions in society, we are social beings meant to be together.

Milestone Goals

- Reflect on your own experiences with connection and community. How have these experiences affected your life?

  _____
  _____
  _____
  _____
  _____

- Consider how the power of connection might change your perspective and lead to growth.

  _____
  _____
  _____
  _____
  _____

- Reflect on your experiences with healing. How can connection contribute to this process?

  _____
  _____

_____
_____
_____

- Think about how you can incorporate the practice of connection into your life.

_____
_____
_____
_____
_____

Action Plan

- Spend some time each day reflecting on your experiences with connection. This could involve journaling, meditation, or simply quiet contemplation.

_____
_____
_____
_____
_____

- If you're facing a challenge, consider seeking support from a counselor or trusted friend.

_____
_____
_____
_____
_____

- Practice connection in your daily life. Notice how this practice affects your emotions and experiences.

_____

_____

_____

_____

_____

- Regularly check in with yourself about your 'juice' levels. If you notice they're running low, take steps to replenish them.

_____

_____

_____

_____

_____

- Embrace the concept of connection in your daily life. Try to see the power of connection in all aspects of your life, even when things seem challenging or fearful.

_____

_____

_____

_____

_____

Chapter 20: Embracing Imperfection

Chapter 20 of "The Well-Lived Life," titled "Embracing Imperfection," discusses the importance of accepting imperfection in life and our interactions with others. McGarey begins the chapter with a story about her son's playdates, contrasting her son's freedom to explore and get dirty with his friend who was kept clean and restrained. This serves as a metaphor for the importance of experiencing life's messiness.

McGarey emphasizes the importance of community and connection, even in the face of imperfection and chaos. She shares her experiences of hosting large gatherings at her home, where the focus was on togetherness rather than maintaining a perfect environment. She discusses the drawbacks of modern conveniences that reduce our need for interaction with others, suggesting that we miss out on the benefits of community when we isolate ourselves.

The chapter concludes with the message that accepting imperfection in our interactions with others can lead to a richer, more fulfilling life. By embracing life's imperfections, we can learn, grow, and find our 'juice' again.

Key Points

- Embrace life's messiness. Accepting imperfection in our interactions with others can lead to a richer, more fulfilling life.

- We thrive when we accept life's imperfections and learn from them.

- By focusing on togetherness rather than a perfect environment, one can find community and connection in the face of imperfection and chaos.

- There are drawbacks to modern conveniences that reduce our need for interaction with others. We miss out on the benefits of community when we isolate ourselves.

Milestone Goals

- Reflect on your own experiences with imperfection and how they have affected your life.

_____

_____

_____

_____

_____

- Consider how embracing imperfection might change your perspective and lead to personal growth.

_____

_____

_____

_____

_____

- Reflect on your experiences with community and connection. How can embracing imperfection enhance these experiences?

_____

_____

_____
_____
_____

- Think about how you can incorporate the acceptance of imperfection into your life.

_____
_____
_____
_____
_____

Action Plan

- Spend some time each day reflecting on your experiences with imperfection. This could involve journaling, meditation, or simply quiet contemplation.

_____
_____
_____
_____
_____

- Practice accepting imperfection in your daily life. Notice how this practice affects your emotions and experiences.

_____
_____
_____
_____
_____

- Regularly check in with yourself about your 'juice' levels. If you notice they're running low, take steps to replenish them.

_____

_____

_____

_____

_____

- Embrace the concept of imperfection in your daily life. Try to see the value in imperfection, even when things seem challenging or chaotic.

_____

_____

_____

_____

_____

Chapter 21: Find Your Friends

Chapter 21 of "The Well-Lived Life," titled "Find Your Friends," explores the importance of building a community of friends and understanding the different types of friendships that can exist. McGarey begins the chapter with a conversation with Elisa, a college student, about the changing nature of friendships. She emphasizes that friendships can evolve, but that doesn't make them any less valuable.

McGarey discusses the concept of being friends with everyone to varying degrees, finding the friend within them regardless of who they are or what they believe. She emphasizes the importance of allowing the universal flow to push new people in your direction and being open to the universe speaking to us through others.

The chapter also highlights the value of interacting with people who think differently from us, as they can push us to see things in a new way. McGarey concludes the chapter with the message that to build a stronger community of friends, start with the people in closest proximity to you and be friends with a wide range of people. By embracing a wide range of friendships, we can enrich our lives and find our 'juice' again.

Key Points

- Friendships can change over time, but that doesn't make them any less valuable.

- You can be friends with everyone to varying degrees, finding the friend within them regardless of who they are or what they believe.

- By allowing the universal flow to push new people in our direction, we allow the universe to speak to us through others.

- There is value in interacting with people who think differently from us, as they can push us to see things in a new way.

- To build a stronger community of friends, start with the people in closest proximity to you and be friends with a wide range of people.

Milestone Goals

- Reflect on your own experiences with friendship and how they have affected your life.

_____

_____

_____

_____

_____

- Consider how embracing a wide range of friendships might change your perspective and lead to personal growth.

_____

_____

_____

_____

_____

- Reflect on your experiences with community and connection. How can embracing a wide range of friendships enhance these experiences?

_____
_____
_____
_____
_____

- Think about how you can incorporate the acceptance of a wide range of friendships into your life.

_____
_____
_____
_____
_____

Action Plan

- Spend some time each day reflecting on your experiences with friends. This could involve journaling, meditation, or simply quiet contemplation.

_____
_____
_____
_____
_____

- Practice accepting a wide range of friendships in your daily life. Notice how this practice affects your emotions and experiences.

_____

_____

_____

_____

_____

- Regularly check in with yourself about your 'juice' levels. If you notice they're running low, take steps to replenish them.

_____

_____

_____

_____

_____

- Embrace the concept of a wide range of friendships in your daily life. Try to see the value in all types of friendships, even when they seem challenging or chaotic.

_____

_____

_____

_____

_____

Chapter 22: How to Set Boundaries

Chapter 22 of "The Well-Lived Life," titled "How to Set Boundaries," delves into the importance of setting healthy boundaries and understanding what gives us energy and what drains it. McGarey begins the chapter by emphasizing the need for self-understanding to set and maintain healthy boundaries.

She shares a story about her sister, Margaret, who was able to set boundaries with her critical mother-in-law by choosing to spend her energy on her child instead of engaging in negative interactions. This story serves as a metaphor for the concept that boundaries are not about keeping people out, but about managing our energy and attention. We can choose to focus on the positive aspects of people and exclude their negative energy.

McGarey also discusses the importance of setting boundaries that contribute to the good of the whole. She shares a story about setting a boundary that led to the formation of the American Society of Clinical Hypnosis: by asking for a weekly meeting to be held somewhere other than her home, she prompted consideration of the group's long-term goals. The chapter concludes with the message that setting boundaries is a part of our soul's journey and can help us and others find the right place in the puzzle of life. By setting appropriate boundaries, we can enrich our lives and find our 'juice' again.

Key Points

- Knowing ourselves well helps us set and maintain healthy boundaries.

- Boundaries help us manage our energy and attention. We can choose to focus on the positive aspects of people and exclude their negative energy.

- Setting good boundaries can contribute to the good of the whole.

- Setting boundaries is a part of our soul's journey and can help us and others find the right place in the puzzle of life.

Milestone Goals

- Reflect on your own experiences with setting boundaries and how they have affected your life.

_____
_____
_____
_____
_____

- Consider how setting healthy boundaries might change your perspective and lead to personal growth.

_____
_____
_____
_____
_____

- Reflect on your experiences with managing your energy and attention. How can setting boundaries enhance these experiences?

_____

_____

_____

_____

_____

- Think about how you can incorporate the practice of
  setting boundaries into your life.

_____

_____

_____

_____

_____

Action Plan

- Spend some time each day reflecting on your
  experiences with setting boundaries. This could
  involve journaling, meditation, or simply quiet
  contemplation.

_____

_____

_____

_____

_____

- Practice setting healthy boundaries in your daily life.
  Notice how this practice affects your emotions and
  experiences.

_____

_____

_____

_____

_____

- Regularly check in with yourself about your 'juice' levels. If you notice they're running low, take steps to replenish them.

_____

_____

_____

_____

_____

- Embrace the concept of setting boundaries in your daily life. Try to see the value in setting boundaries, even when it seems challenging.

_____

_____

_____

_____

_____

Chapter 23: The Power of Listening

Chapter 23 of "The Well-Lived Life," titled "The Power of Listening," emphasizes the importance of active listening in building connections and understanding others. McGarey begins the chapter by discussing her relationship with her sister, Margaret, and how their deep conversations and mutual understanding strengthened their bond.

She also discusses the role of listening in her medical practice, stating that many of her patients, especially women, had never been truly heard by an authority figure before. This listening allowed her to better understand and address their needs. McGarey shares her experiences in Afghanistan, where listening to the women's birth stories helped identify the issues leading to high infant-maternal death rates. This experience underscores the power of listening in understanding and solving problems.

The chapter concludes with the message that listening is a powerful tool for building connections, understanding others, and solving problems. By actively listening, we can strengthen our relationships, better understand the people around us, and find our 'juice' again.

Key Points

- Listening is essential in building strong relationships.

- In positions of authority, listening can help one to understand people's needs and address them accordingly.

- Listening is vital to understanding and solving problems, helping you keenly identify issues.

- Listening can foster a sense of belonging and understanding among members of a community.

Milestone Goals

- Reflect on your own experiences with listening and how they have affected your relationships.

_____

_____

_____

_____

_____

- Consider how improving your listening skills might enhance your understanding of others and lead to personal growth.

_____

_____

_____

_____

_____

- Reflect on your experiences with community and connection. How can active listening enhance these experiences?

_____

_____

_____

- Think about how you can incorporate the practice of active listening into your daily life.

_____
_____
_____
_____
_____

Action Plan

- Spend some time each day practicing active listening. This could involve engaging in deep conversations with friends or family or simply paying more attention to the people around you.

_____
_____
_____
_____
_____

- Practice active listening in your daily interactions. Notice how this practice affects your relationships and understanding of others.

_____
_____
_____
_____
_____

- Regularly check in with yourself about your 'juice' levels. If you notice they're running low, take steps to replenish them.

- Embrace the concept of active listening in your daily life. Try to see the value in truly understanding others, even when it seems challenging.

Chapter 24: Angels Appear

Chapter 24 of "The Well-Lived Life," titled "Angels Appear," underscores the power of community and the importance of reciprocal relationships. McGarey begins the chapter with a story about her Aunt Belle, who, despite having no cow, built a cowshed in her orphanage in India, believing that a cow would come - and it did.

McGarey shares her own experience of faith and community during her time in medical school. Despite having no money to prepare a Thanksgiving meal, she invited friends over, trusting that something would work out - and it did, thanks to her neighbors.

She also shares a story about her time at Deaconess Hospital, where a kind cleaner named Lucille secretly changed the surgery schedule to give McGarey more rest. This act of kindness underscores the importance of supporting and being supported by the community.

The chapter concludes with the message that when we commit to our life force and feed it through community, angels appear to ease us along the path. By contributing to the collective life force, we can trust that it will support us in return.

Key Points

- Community is a give-and-take relationship. By contributing to the collective life force, we can trust that it will support us in return.

- When we commit to our life force and feed it through community, angels appear to ease us along the path.

Milestone Goals

- Reflect on your own experiences with community and support. How have these experiences affected your life?

_____
_____
_____
_____
_____

- Consider how being more active in your community might enhance your sense of belonging and lead to personal growth.

_____
_____
_____
_____
_____

- Reflect on your experiences with faith and trust. How can these experiences enhance your relationship with your community?

_____
_____
_____
_____
_____

- Think about how you can incorporate the practice of giving and taking into your daily life.

_____
_____
_____
_____
_____

Action Plan

- Spend some time each day reflecting on your experiences with community and support. This could involve journaling, meditation, or simply quiet contemplation.

_____
_____
_____
_____
_____

- Practice giving and taking in your daily interactions. Notice how this practice affects your relationships and sense of community.

_____
_____
_____
_____
_____

- Regularly check in with yourself about your 'juice' levels. If you notice they're running low, take steps to replenish them.

_____

_____

_____

_____

_____

- Embrace the concept of community in your daily life. Try to see the value in supporting and being supported by others, even when it seems challenging.

_____

_____

_____

_____

_____

Chapter 25 of "The Well-Lived Life," titled "A Lesson in Everything," emphasizes the importance of learning from life's experiences and the power of gratitude. McGarey shares her personal experience of deciding to stop driving due to deteriorating eyesight, which she took as a sign from life that it was time to make a change.

The chapter underscores that life is always trying to teach us something, communicating with us through events, people, and ideas, and offering us opportunities for gratitude. McGarey also discusses the concept of "toxic positivity" and differentiates it from true optimism. True optimism involves acknowledging pain and challenges while still looking for the positive aspects or lessons in each situation.

The chapter concludes with the message that even in difficult moments, there are lessons to be learned and opportunities for gratitude. By embracing the concept of learning from everything, we can enhance our personal growth and replenish our 'juice'.

Key Points

- Life's process consists of tiny moments and minuscule choices that shape our self-understanding and our role in the world.

- Life constantly offers lessons through events, people, and ideas, providing opportunities for gratitude.

- To differentiate toxic positivity from true optimism, it's crucial to acknowledge pain and challenges while still seeking the positive aspects or lessons in each situation.

Milestone Goals

- Reflect on your own experiences and the lessons you've learned from them.

_____
_____
_____
_____
_____

- Consider how acknowledging life's lessons and expressing gratitude can enhance your personal growth.

_____
_____
_____
_____
_____

- Reflect on your experiences with challenges and how they have shaped your understanding of life.

_____
_____
_____
_____
_____

- Think about how you can incorporate the practice of learning from everything into your daily life.

_____
_____
_____
_____
_____

Action Plan

- Spend some time each day reflecting on your experiences and the lessons you've learned from them.

_____
_____
_____
_____
_____

- Practice acknowledging life's lessons and expressing gratitude in your daily interactions.

_____
_____
_____
_____
_____

- Regularly check in with yourself about your 'juice' levels. If you notice they're running low, take steps to replenish them.

_____

_____

_____

_____

_____

- Embrace the concept of learning from everything in your daily life. Try to see the value in every experience, even when it seems challenging.

_____

_____

_____

_____

_____

Chapter 26: How to Stop Fighting

Chapter 26 of "The Well-Lived Life," titled "How to Stop Fighting," explores the concept of embracing life's challenges rather than resisting them. McGarey begins the chapter by sharing her transformation from a fighter to a person who engages positively with life. This transformation was inspired by her mother's approach to life's challenges, which was not to fight them but to engage with them and learn from them.

McGarey also introduces the concept of people who are like silk - strong yet flexible due to their deep self-love. These individuals contrast with those who constantly fight life's challenges, often draining their energy in the process.

The chapter concludes with the idea that challenges are not punishments but opportunities for growth. McGarey recounts the story of psychiatrist and psychotherapist Dr. Milton Erickson, whose interest in consciousness developed through his battle with polio. Dr. Erickson learned profound lessons about the human mind and nervous system and created a lasting legacy in his field. His story is a testament to how engaging with a situation rather than fighting a circumstance can produce powerful results. McGarey emphasizes that it's through pain and struggle that significant life changes often occur, pushing us forward on our life's journey.

Key Points

- Life's challenges are not punishments but opportunities for growth and learning.

- Redirecting energy towards engaging with life, especially during tough times, can be highly rewarding, providing direction and learning opportunities.

- McGarey differentiates between people with deep self-love who are strong yet flexible, like silk, and those who constantly fight life's challenges.

- Challenges push us forward, and it's through pain and struggle that significant life changes often occur.

Milestone Goals

- Reflect on your own experiences with challenges and how they have shaped your life.

_____

_____

_____

_____

_____

- Consider how a shift in perspective from fighting to engaging with life could impact your personal growth.

_____

_____

_____

_____

_____

- Reflect on your approach to life's challenges and how it affects your energy levels.

_____

_____

_____

_____

_____

- Think about how you can incorporate the practice of engaging with life, especially during tough times, into your daily life.

_____

_____

_____

_____

_____

Action Plan

- Spend some time each day reflecting on your experiences with challenges and the lessons you've learned from them.

_____

_____

_____

_____

_____

- Practice engaging with life's challenges in a positive way, redirecting your energy toward learning and growth.

_____

_____

_____

_____

_____

- Regularly check in with yourself about your 'juice' levels. If you notice they're running low, take steps to replenish them.

_____

_____

_____

_____

_____

- Embrace the concept of engaging with life, especially during tough times, in your daily life. Try to see the value in every challenge, even when it seems difficult.

_____

_____

_____

_____

_____

Chapter 27: The Role of Dreams

Chapter 27 of "The Well-Lived Life," titled "The Role of Dreams," delves into the significance of dreams as a communication channel between our subconscious and conscious minds. McGarey shares a poignant story of a woman tormented by a recurring nightmare. This woman, who had lost her children to her abusive ex-husband, was haunted by a dream where her attempts to protect her children resulted in their harm. Over time, she realized that the dream was a reflection of her hatred for her ex-husband consuming her energy, energy that could be better spent on love for her children. This realization led her to redirect her energy towards something constructive, illustrating the power of dreams in guiding our actions and perspectives.

McGarey emphasizes that dreams can offer clarity to questions that feel too big for the conscious mind to handle. She encourages readers to request guidance from their dreams and be open to the messages they might convey. The interpretation of dreams, she notes, is personal and subjective, often involving symbolism that is unique to the dreamer. The chapter concludes with the idea that whether dreams signify help from beyond or simply from the obscure recesses of ourselves, they can be of enormous assistance.

Key Points

- Dreams serve as a communication channel between our subconscious and conscious minds, often providing insights and guidance.

- Dreams can offer clarity to questions that feel too big for the conscious mind to handle.

- Requesting a dream and being ready to receive it can open up avenues for guidance.

- The interpretation of dreams is personal and subjective, often involving symbolism that is unique to the dreamer.

Milestone Goals

- Reflect on your dreams and consider what they might be trying to communicate.

_____
_____
_____
_____
_____

- Consider how a shift in perspective, as illustrated by the woman's story, could impact your personal growth.

_____
_____
_____
_____
_____

- Reflect on the symbols in your dreams and what they might mean to you.

_____
_____

_____
_____
_____

- Think about how you can incorporate the practice of requesting and interpreting dreams into your daily life.

_____
_____
_____
_____
_____

Action Plan

- Keep a dream journal to record and reflect on your dreams.

_____
_____
_____
_____
_____

- Practice interpreting the symbols in your dreams, keeping in mind that the interpretation is personal and subjective.

_____
_____
_____
_____
_____

- Regularly request guidance from your dreams and be open to the messages they might convey.

_____

_____

_____

_____

_____

- Embrace the concept of using dreams as a source of guidance and wisdom in your daily life.

_____

_____

_____

_____

_____

Chapter 28: When You Just Keep Hurting

Chapter 28 of "The Well-Lived Life," titled "When You Just Keep Hurting," explores the concept of chronic pain and how one's perspective can influence their experience with it. McGarey shares the story of Sarit, a woman who experienced chronic shoulder pain due to long hours at the computer. Sarit discovered that her pain was linked to her suppressed desire to dance, a passion she had neglected since childhood (she had used her right shoulder to pitch during her years playing softball, a sport her father wanted her to play). By integrating dance into her daily routine, Sarit's shoulder began to release, illustrating the power of perspective in managing chronic pain.

McGarey also shares the story of Evelyn, a friend who paints her way through flare-ups of chronic pain, finding joy and release in the process. This story highlights how chronic pain can inform activities that give individuals meaning and help them manage their pain.

The chapter also discusses the experiences of two women with lupus, Janet and Laura. Janet, who adopted a positive attitude and learned to live a more balanced life, had a different experience than Laura, who felt stuck and focused more on her lupus than her life. One's attitude towards their condition can influence their experience with it.

McGarey concludes the chapter by emphasizing that chronic pain can serve as a teacher, guiding us to shift our perspective and learn from our circumstances. She encourages readers to view their pain as a teacher rather than an enemy and to use it to guide their actions and perspectives in their daily life.

Key Points

- Chronic pain can serve as a teacher, guiding us to shift our perspective and learn from our circumstances.

- Physical pain can sometimes be linked to unmet psychological needs or desires.

- Chronic conditions often include repetitive symptoms that follow the same pattern each time. Changing how we think about pain can interrupt that pattern and have a significant effect.

- Some people with chronic pain can let their pain inform a certain activity that gives them meaning.

Milestone Goals

- Reflect on your own experiences with pain or discomfort and consider what they might be trying to communicate.

_____

_____

_____

_____

_____

- Consider how a shift in perspective, as illustrated by Sarit's story, could impact your personal growth.

_____

_____

_____

_____

_____

- Reflect on how you can incorporate the practice of learning from your pain into your daily life.

_____

_____

_____

_____

_____

- Think about how you can redirect your focus from your pain to your life, as Janet did.

_____

_____

_____

_____

_____

Action Plan

- Keep a journal to record and reflect on your experiences with pain.

_____

_____

_____

_____

_____

- Practice shifting your perspective towards your pain, viewing it as a teacher rather than an enemy.

- Regularly take time to engage in an activity that brings you joy and helps you manage your pain, like Evelyn's painting.

- Embrace the concept of learning from your pain and using it to guide your actions and perspectives in your daily life

---

Chapter 29: In the Impossible Moments

Chapter 29 of "The Well-Lived Life," titled "In the Impossible Moments," delves into the concept of dealing with deep emotional pain and betrayal. McGarey shares her personal experience of her husband leaving her for another woman, a nurse at their clinic, after 46 years of marriage. This event was deeply painful and shocking for McGarey, who had believed in their partnership and commitment to each other.

Despite the pain, McGarey emphasizes the importance of shifting perspective during such painful experiences, viewing them as opportunities for growth and learning. She shares how she managed to navigate through this difficult period by listening to her inner wisdom, which she refers to as "Dr. Gladys." This inner wisdom guided her to seek out teachings from her experiences and to find a way to be grateful despite the pain.

McGarey also shares how she started a new clinic with her daughter after the divorce, symbolizing a new beginning. She encourages readers to listen to their inner wisdom during challenging times and to seek out teachings from their experiences. The chapter concludes with the idea that healing is an ongoing process, and as we move forward, we can extract more and more from the pain of the past.

Key Points

- Deep emotional pain and betrayal can serve as catalysts for personal growth and transformation.

- Personal experiences, such as McGarey's divorce after 46 years of marriage, can lead to profound shifts in perspective.

- Shifting perspective during painful experiences can transform them into opportunities for growth and learning.

- Listening to one's inner wisdom during challenging times can provide guidance and insights.

- Seeking teachings from personal experiences can lead to a deeper understanding and appreciation of life's journey.

Milestone Goals

- Reflect on a personal experience of deep emotional pain or betrayal and how it has shaped you.

_____

_____

_____

_____

_____

- Identify your inner wisdom or guiding voice that helps you navigate through challenging times.

_____

_____

_____

_____

_____

- Consider a painful experience in your life and try to shift your perspective on it, viewing it as an opportunity for growth and learning.

_____
_____
_____
_____
_____

- Think about a new beginning or opportunity that emerged from a painful or challenging experience in your life.

_____
_____
_____
_____
_____

Action Plan

- Spend some time in quiet reflection or journaling about a personal experience of deep emotional pain or betrayal.

_____
_____
_____
_____
_____

- Try to identify your inner wisdom or guiding voice. What does it sound like? When does it speak to you?

_____

_____

_____

_____

_____

- Choose a painful experience in your life and try to shift your perspective on it. Write down what you learned from this experience and how it has contributed to your growth.

_____

_____

_____

_____

_____

- Reflect on a new beginning or opportunity that emerged from a painful or challenging experience. How did this new beginning help you move forward?

_____

_____

_____

_____

_____

- Continue to listen to your inner wisdom as you navigate through life's challenges. Remember that healing is an ongoing process and that you can continue to learn and grow from your experiences.

_____

_____

_____

Chapter 30: Lesson After Lesson

Chapter 30 of "The Well-Lived Life," titled "Lesson After Lesson," delves into the idea that life's lessons often come through challenging experiences and in their own time. McGarey shares her journey of learning from her divorce, which she initially saw as a devastating event. Over time, she came to understand that her ex-husband's desire to be with someone else was reason enough for them not to be together. She also realized that she had suppressed her own needs and identity to be the wife she thought he needed, which had taken a toll on her soul's mission.

McGarey also discusses the importance of not identifying with our struggles. She shares the contrasting experiences of two of her patients with lupus. One patient, Janet, did not identify with her pain or her lupus, which allowed her to manage her symptoms effectively. In contrast, the other patient, Laura, identified strongly with her lupus, even displaying it on her car's license plate, and continued to suffer greatly from her symptoms.

The chapter emphasizes the power of shifting our perspective during challenging times and viewing these times as opportunities for growth and learning. McGarey encourages readers to ask themselves what they can learn from their experiences and to express gratitude, even amid challenges. She concludes the chapter with a series of steps to help readers find the lessons in their challenges, including asking for a dream to provide insight, interpreting the dream, expressing gratitude for any lessons found, and expressing gratitude to oneself for seeking out the lesson.

Key Points

- Life's lessons come in their own time and often through challenging experiences.

- Identifying ourselves with our struggles can hinder our growth and healing process.

- Shifting our perspective and asking ourselves what we can learn from our experiences can transform our struggles into opportunities for growth.

- It's important to separate our identities from our struggles and not let them define us.

- Expressing gratitude, even amid challenges, can help us maintain a positive perspective and open us up to life's teachings.

Milestone Goals

- Reflect on a challenging experience and identify what lessons it might have taught you.

_____
_____
_____
_____
_____

- Consider how you identify with your struggles and think about how you can separate your identity from them.

_____
_____

_____

_____

_____

- Practice shifting your perspective during a difficult situation and ask yourself what you can learn from it.

_____

_____

_____

_____

- Express gratitude daily, even when facing challenges, and observe how this practice affects your perspective and emotional state.

_____

_____

_____

_____

Action Plan

- Reflect on a challenging experience in your life and write down what lessons it taught you.

_____

_____

_____

_____

- Identify a struggle that you feel defines you and brainstorm ways to separate your identity from this struggle.

_____
_____
_____
_____
_____

- The next time you face a difficult situation, pause and ask yourself what you can learn from it. Write down your thoughts.

_____
_____
_____
_____
_____

- Start a gratitude journal and write down three things you're grateful for each day, even on difficult days.

_____
_____
_____
_____
_____

- Review your journal entries at the end of each week and reflect on how this practice has affected your perspective and emotional state.

_____
_____

Secret VI: Spend Your Energy Wildly
Chapter 31: Energy As An Investment

Chapter 31 of "The Well-Lived Life," titled "Energy As An Investment," delves into the concept of life as energy and the importance of directing this energy towards life. McGarey explains that our life force is the directional aspect of this energy, and learning to steer our energy toward life is key to living well. She emphasizes that energy is neither created nor destroyed, it merely changes shape, and when we align our energy with life, we create a give-and-take relationship with the source.

The chapter also explores the concept of fear, particularly the fear of not having enough, which can block the flow of life force. McGarey suggests that this fear often stems from past experiences and can be passed down through generations. She encourages readers to shift their perspective from a mindset of scarcity to one of abundance, asking themselves what they have enough of and what they can give to receive.

McGarey concludes the chapter by encouraging readers to view their energy as an investment. By investing our energy in life, we can borrow it back when we're running low. This concept is not about cognitive wisdom but about the wisdom of our wildness, the wisdom of our bodies, and the wisdom of the cycles of the universe.

Key Points

- Life itself is energy, and living well involves learning how to direct this energy toward life.

- Energy is neither created nor destroyed; it merely changes shape. Our life force is the directional aspect of this energy.

- We can consciously invest our life force in what gives it back to us, creating a continuous flow of positivity and light.

- Fear of not having enough can block the flow of life force. Overcoming this fear involves shifting our perspective and focusing on what we do have enough of.

- Energy should be viewed as an investment. By investing our energy in life, we can borrow it back when we're running low.

Milestone Goals

- Reflect on how you currently direct your energy in your life. Are there areas where you could redirect your energy towards more life-affirming activities or thoughts?

_____
_____
_____
_____
_____

- Identify a fear or worry that you have about not having enough of something (time, money, love, etc.). Consider how this fear might be blocking your life force.

_____
_____
_____
_____
_____

- Practice shifting your perspective from a mindset of scarcity to one of abundance. What do you have enough of? What can you give to receive?

_____
_____
_____
_____
_____

- Consider how you can invest your energy in ways that give it back to you. What activities, relationships, or thoughts energize you and make you feel more alive?

_____
_____
_____
_____
_____

Action Plan

- Make a list of areas in your life where you feel your energy is being drained. Next to each item, write down a way you could redirect your energy towards something more life-affirming.

_____
_____
_____
_____
_____

- Write down a fear or worry you have about not having enough of something. Reflect on how this fear might be blocking your life force and write down one action you could take to overcome this fear.

_____
_____
_____
_____
_____

- Each day for a week, write down three things that you have enough of. At the end of the week, reflect on how this practice has shifted your perspective.

_____
_____
_____
_____
_____

- Make a list of activities, relationships, or thoughts that energize you and make you feel more alive. Commit to investing more of your energy in these areas.

_____
_____
_____

Chapter 32: What's Worth Your Energy?

Chapter 32 of "The Well-Lived Life," titled "What's Worth Your Energy?" delves into the concept of energy as a resource that should be directed towards what we love most. McGarey also discusses the importance of rest as a natural part of the rhythm of life. She explains that true rest is an action, not just the absence of doing anything. It involves thinking kind, gentle, regenerative thoughts about our body and being fully present. She shares her personal experience of how her sleep patterns have changed as she aged, and how she uses her awake time at night to focus on what brings her joy and happiness.

The chapter concludes with the idea that giving life our "all" can sometimes lead to fear of not having enough, but it's in these moments that wondrous things can happen. McGarey encourages readers to embrace these moments and to remember that as long as they still have energy left, it's up to them to keep spending it on what brings them joy.

Key Points

- Energy should be directed towards what we love most, as it helps us turn towards life and receive the energy that is waiting for us.

- Rest is a natural part of the rhythm of life, and it's during rest that we rejuvenate our energy.

- True rest is an action, not just the absence of doing anything. It involves thinking kind, gentle, regenerative thoughts about our body and being fully present.

- Giving life our "all" can sometimes lead to fear of not having enough, but it's in these moments that wondrous things can happen.

Milestone Goals

- Reflect on where you direct your energy. Are there areas in your life where you could redirect your energy toward what you love most?

_____
_____
_____
_____
_____

- Consider your rhythm of rest. Are there changes you could make to better rejuvenate your energy?

_____
_____
_____
_____
_____

- Practice true rest by dedicating time to thinking kind, gentle, regenerative thoughts about your body and being fully present.

_____
_____
_____
_____
_____

- Reflect on moments when you've given life your "all". What wondrous things happened?

_____
_____
_____
_____
_____

Action Plan

- Make a list of what you love most in life. Each day, try to direct your energy towards one of these things.

_____
_____
_____
_____
_____

- Set aside time each day for true rest. Use this time to think kind, gentle, regenerative thoughts about your body and be fully present.

_____
_____
_____
_____
_____

- Reflect on a moment when you've given life your "all". Write down what happened and how it made you feel.

_____

_____

_____

_____

_____

- Each night before bed, reflect on how you directed your energy that day. Did you direct it toward what you love most? How can you improve tomorrow?

_____

_____

_____

_____

_____

Chapter 33: Making Space for Miracles

Chapter 33, "Making Space for Miracles," delves into the idea of investing energy in what truly matters in life. McGarey uses the story of her Aunt Belle, who lived her life with the belief that whatever she gave away with an open heart would return to her, to illustrate the concept of energy flow. Aunt Belle came back one day with badly worn down shoes because she had traded the new shoes Aunt Mary had just bought for her with the shoes of her new friend who was living on the street (Aunt Mary bought her new shoes a second time). McGarey emphasizes that it's only when we give all we've got that life starts to send energy back to us.

McGarey also discusses the importance of taking measured risks and investing energy in things that bring joy and meaning. She shares the stories of Bobbie and Susan, two women who used their struggles to identify what mattered to their unique souls and spent their energy on that, resulting in rich and incredible lives.

The chapter concludes with the idea that understanding what is worth each person's energy varies from individual to individual and from moment to moment. McGarey encourages readers to listen to their inner knowing to discern how and where to invest their life force.

Key Points

- Energy flows back to us when we give all we've got.

- Taking measured risks and investing energy in things that bring joy and meaning is important.

- Understanding what is worth each person's energy varies from individual to individual and from moment to moment.

- Listening to our inner knowing helps us discern how and where to invest our life force.

Milestone Goals

- Identify what truly matters in your life and invest your energy there.

_____

_____

_____

_____

_____

- Be willing to take measured risks for things that bring joy and meaning.

_____

_____

_____

_____

_____

- Practice listening to your inner knowing to guide your energy investments.

_____

_____

_____

_____

_____

Action Plan

- Reflect on what truly matters to you and where you want to invest your energy.

  _____
  _____
  _____
  _____
  _____

- Identify areas in your life where you can take measured risks to bring more joy and meaning.

  _____
  _____
  _____
  _____
  _____

- Practice mindfulness or meditation to enhance your ability to listen to your inner knowing.

  _____
  _____
  _____
  _____
  _____

- Regularly reassess your energy investments to ensure they align with your values and goals.

  _____
  _____
  _____

Chapter 34: Feeding the Positive

Chapter 34 of "The Well-Lived Life," titled "Feeding the Positive," discusses the importance of investing energy in positive aspects of life. McGarey uses her personal experience of dealing with her divorce to illustrate this concept. She shares a dream she had where her family cut silver ropes that symbolized negativity, freeing her from the emotional burden she carried. This dream led her to consciously invest positive energy into her memories with her ex-husband, focusing on the good times they had together rather than the pain of their separation.

McGarey also shares stories of people who managed to find positivity in challenging situations. She recounts the story of a friend who turned her small apartment into a green oasis after missing her large yard and a patient named Eric who managed to find joy in his office job after initially enjoying working from home during the Covid-19 pandemic. These stories underline the idea that it's not always the external circumstances that need to change for us to be happy, but rather an internal shift in attention.

Key Points

- Investing energy in positive aspects of life can lead to personal growth and happiness.

- Consciously investing positive energy into certain memories can help us redirect the pain associated with them.

- It's not always the external circumstances that need to change for us to be happy, but rather an internal shift in attention.

- McGarey shares stories of people who managed to find positivity in challenging situations, emphasizing the power of perspective and positive energy investment.

Milestone Goals

- Identify areas in your life where you can shift your energy investment from negative to positive aspects.

_____
_____
_____
_____
_____

- Practice conscious energy investment in positive memories and experiences.

_____
_____
_____
_____
_____

- Make an internal shift in attention to focus on the positive aspects of challenging situations.

_____
_____
_____
_____
_____

Action Plan

- Reflect on your personal experiences and identify areas where you have been investing negative energy.

  _____
  _____
  _____
  _____
  _____

- Consciously decide to shift your energy towards the positive aspects of these experiences.

  _____
  _____
  _____
  _____
  _____

- Practice this shift in daily life, focusing on the positive aspects of challenging situations.

  _____
  _____
  _____
  _____
  _____

- Reflect on the changes in your feelings and overall happiness as you make this shift.

  _____
  _____
  _____

Chapter 35: Shifting Your Attention

Chapter 35 of "The Well-Lived Life," titled "Shifting Your Attention," discusses the importance of directing our energy towards things that matter and bring joy. McGarey shares the story of Barry, a patient diagnosed with chronic fatigue syndrome. Barry, who had been living a life of caution and fear due to his mother's risk-averse nature, was encouraged by McGarey to shift his perspective on how he spent his energy. Instead of conserving it, Barry was advised to invest his energy in activities that brought him joy and fulfillment. Barry began writing stories, exploring new places, and cycling again, activities that rejuvenated his energy and made his life feel full. The chapter emphasizes the importance of embracing life and investing our energy in activities that enhance our life force.

Key Points

- Energy should be directed towards things that matter and bring joy.

- Shifting perspective on how we spend our energy can lead to a more fulfilling life.

- Investing energy in activities that enhance our life force can rejuvenate us.

- Embracing life and its challenges can lead to a more fulfilling and energetic life.

Milestone Goals

- Consider the activities, people, and places you've put energy into throughout your life. Identify what has drained your energy and where you can invest your energy for a return.

_____
_____
_____
_____
_____

- Try to get out of your thinking mind for a moment and feel. Let your thoughts wander over those same activities, people, and places in your life, but this time, instead of just thinking about them, feel them. Does your energy flow freely or shrink back? Do you feel an increase or a decrease in your life force?

_____
_____
_____
_____
_____

- Based on what you felt in step 2, consciously pick one activity, person, or place that brings you more energy. How could you invite more of that into your life? Could you practice that activity more often, give that person a call, or spend more time in that place? Find one small shift you could make and move toward it.

_____
_____
_____

_____

_____

- Thinking of step 2 again, consider the people, places, and activities that drain your energy. Look for at least one thing you can just stop doing completely. Pick something small to start. What would it take to just give this up? Could you do it with gratitude and love?

_____

_____

_____

_____

_____

- Then consider the things that are draining your energy but that you don't want or aren't able to release. How can you change the way you spend your life force? Can you change the way you think about that person, can you adjust the way you spend time in that place, or can you shift the type of energy you put into that activity?

_____

_____

_____

_____

_____

Action Plan

- Start by identifying activities, people, and places that drain your energy and those that enhance it.

_____

_____

_____

_____

_____

- Make a conscious effort to invest more energy in activities, people, and places that enhance your life force.

_____

_____

_____

_____

_____

- Identify at least one activity that drains your energy and make a plan to stop doing it completely.

_____

_____

_____

_____

_____

- For activities that drain your energy but can't be completely abandoned, find ways to change how you approach them. This could involve changing your mindset or adjusting how you spend your time.

_____

_____

_____

_____

_____

- Embrace life and its challenges, and be open to the lessons they bring. This involves opening your arms wide and imagining yourself embracing the force of life, feeling life's boundless energy moving out from your heart and through your fingertips. Practice this first thing in the morning or just before going to bed, allowing yourself to embrace the wildness of life all around you.

_____

_____

_____

_____

_____

Background Information About *The Well-Lived Life*

"*The Well-Lived Life*" by Gladys McGarey was published in 2023. The book is divided into 35 chapters, each presenting a unique lesson or perspective on living a fulfilling and meaningful life. The book is a compilation of McGarey's personal experiences, insights, and wisdom gained over her lifetime.

In "The Well-Lived Life," McGarey shares her journey of self-discovery and personal growth, offering readers a roadmap to navigate their own life's challenges and opportunities. The book encourages readers to shift their perspective on life's trials, viewing them not as obstacles but as opportunities for growth and learning.

McGarey's book is more than just a memoir; it's a guide to living a well-lived life. Through her personal stories and insights, she provides practical advice and strategies to help readers embrace life's challenges, invest their energy wisely, and create a life of joy and fulfillment.

"The Well-Lived Life" is a testament to McGarey's belief in the power of self-love, resilience, and the human spirit. It's a book that encourages readers to live their life to the fullest, to embrace their unique journey, and to find joy and fulfillment in every moment.

"The Well-Lived Life" will inspire you to view your life's challenges as opportunities for growth, to invest your energy in what truly matters, and to live a life of joy, fulfillment, and purpose.

Background Information About Dr. Gladys McGarey

Gladys McGarey is a renowned holistic medicine practitioner, author, and speaker. Known as the "Mother of Holistic Medicine," McGarey has dedicated her life to promoting a holistic approach to health and wellness, emphasizing the interconnectedness of the mind, body, and spirit.

Born in India to medical missionary parents in 1920, McGarey's exposure to diverse cultures and healing practices from a young age shaped her holistic view of medicine. She came to the United States in 1935 to attend college and medical school and has been in practice for over 70 years.

In 1978, she co-founded the American Holistic Medical Association, an organization that promotes holistic and integrative medicine. She also established the Foundation for Living Medicine, a non-profit organization that spreads knowledge and supports the holistic health movement.

Throughout her career, McGarey has been a pioneer in her field, introducing concepts such as birthing centers and the use of acupuncture in the United States. She has worked tirelessly to promote a shift in the medical paradigm, advocating for a more holistic and integrative approach to healthcare.

As an author, McGarey has written several books, including "The Physician Within You" and "Born to Live." Her latest book, "The Well-Lived Life," is a testament to her belief in the power of self-love, resilience, and the human spirit.

Gladys McGarey's work has had a profound impact on the field of holistic medicine, and her teachings continue to inspire and guide individuals on their journey to health and wellness. She currently lives in Scottsdale, Arizona, and recently became a great-great-grandmother.

Trivia Questions

1. What is the title of the first chapter of the book?

2. What is the significance of the term "juice" as used by McGarey in the book?

3. How many chapters are there in "The Well-Lived Life"?

4. What undertaking serves as a new beginning for McGarey after her divorce, as discussed in Chapter 29?

5. Who is Barry and what is his significance in the book?

6. What is the concept of people being like silk as discussed in the book?

7. What is the title of the last chapter in the book?

8. What is the main theme of Chapter 24, "Angels Appear"?

9. For how many years was McGarey married to her ex-husband Bill?

10. What personal transformation does McGarey discuss in Chapter 26, "How to Stop Fighting"?

11. What is the significance of dreams in McGarey's book?

12. Why did Aunt Mary buy Aunt Belle a pair of new shoes for the second time in Chapter 33, "Making Space for Miracles"?

13. What is the concept of "Feeding the Positive" as discussed in Chapter 34?

14. What is the significance of the story of Dr. Milton Erickson in the book?

15. What is the key message of Chapter 27, "The Role of Dreams"?

16. What is the significance of the silver ropes in McGarey's dream as discussed in the book?

Deeper Analysis of the Themes in The Well-Lived Life

"The Well-Lived Life" by Gladys McGarey is a profound exploration of the human experience, filled with wisdom and insights that challenge readers to live their lives to the fullest. The book delves into several key themes that are worth exploring in more depth:

1. **The Power of Perspective**: Throughout the book, McGarey emphasizes the importance of perspective. She encourages readers to view life's challenges not as obstacles but as opportunities for growth and learning. This shift in perspective can transform our experiences and lead to a more fulfilling and meaningful life.

2. **The Importance of Self-Love**: Self-love is a recurring theme in "The Well-Lived Life." McGarey discusses the concept of people who are like silk - strong yet flexible due to their deep self-love. She encourages readers to cultivate self-love, as it can serve as a source of strength and resilience in the face of life's challenges.

3. **The Role of Energy**: Energy is another key theme in the book. McGarey discusses the concept of investing our energy wisely, directing it towards things that matter and bring joy. She argues that how we spend our energy can significantly impact our life's quality and fulfillment.

4. **The Value of Dreams**: Dreams play a significant role in "The Well-Lived Life." McGarey shares her dreams and their interpretations, emphasizing the importance of dreams as a source of guidance and insight. She encourages readers to pay attention to their dreams and to seek out their teachings.

5. **The Journey of Personal Growth**: The book is, at its core, a journey of personal growth. McGarey shares her journey of transformation and growth, offering readers a roadmap to navigate their own life's challenges and opportunities. She emphasizes that personal growth often comes through pain and struggle, pushing us forward on our life's journey.

By exploring these themes, "The Well-Lived Life" offers readers a guide to living a fulfilling and meaningful life. It encourages us to shift our perspective, cultivate self-love, invest our energy wisely, value our dreams, and embrace the journey of personal growth.

More books from Smart Reads

Summary of Breath: The New Science of a Lost Art By
    James Nestor
Workbook for What Happened to You? By Oprah Winfrey
    and Dr. Bruce Perry
Workbook for Limitless By Jim Kwik
Workbook for The Body Keeps the Score By Dr. Bessel van
    der Kolk
Workbook for Atlas of the Heart By Brené Brown
Workbook for Fast Like a Girl By Dr. Mindy Pelz
Workbook for The Tools By Phil Stutz and Barry Michels
Workbook for Glucose Revolution By Jessie Inchauspe
Workbook for Forgiving What You Can't Forget by Lysa
    TerKeurst
Workbook for Adult Children of Emotionally Immature
    Parents by Lindsay C. Gibson

Thank You

Hope you've enjoyed your reading experience.

We here at Smart Reads will always strive to deliver to you the highest quality guides.

So I'd like to thank you for supporting us and reading until the very end.

Before you go, would you mind leaving us a review on Amazon?

It will mean a lot to us and support us creating high quality guides for you in the future.

Thanks once again!

Warmly yours,

The Smart Reads Team

Download Your Free Gift

As a way to say "Thank You" for being a fan of our series, I've included a free gift for you:

Brain Health: How to Nurture and Nourish Your Brain For Top Performance

Go to www.smart-reads.com to get your FREE book.

The Smart Reads Team

Made in the USA
Las Vegas, NV
20 May 2024

90161579R00098